THE VOYAGES OF
CAPTAIN COOK

Jason Hook

Illustrated by Richard Hook

Great Journeys

Cover *The voyages of Captain James Cook (1728–79) earned him a place among the greatest navigators in history. He travelled through iceberg-ridden waters to the heat of South-Pacific Islands.*

Frontispiece *Cook is shown here, in uniform, studying his charts.*

Editor: Tracey Smith
Series designer: Ross George

First published in 1990 by
Wayland (Publishers) Limited
61 Western Road, Hove
East Sussex, BN3 1JD, England

Typeset by R. Gibbs & N. Taylor, Wayland
Printed in Italy by G.Canale & C.S.p.A., Turin
Bound in Belgium by Casterman, S.A.

British Library Cataloguing in Publication Data
Hook, Jason
    The voyages of Captain Cook.
    1. Exploration voyages by Cook, James, 1728–1770
    I. Title II. Hook, Richard   III. Series
910.45

ISBN 1–85210–330–2

Contents

A Secret Task

By the sixteenth century, the tiny ships of Europe's ocean explorers had conquered the Atlantic Ocean, and sailed east beyond Africa to gather the precious spices of the Indies. The Pacific Ocean, though, which covers a larger surface area than all the lands of the Earth combined, was still unknown space on the map of the globe.

In 1520, the Portuguese sailor Ferdinand Magellan made the first Pacific crossing. Other explorers soon followed his example, including the Dutchman Abel Tasman who charted New Zealand in 1642 and Australia two years later. With each voyage, rumours grew of the existence of a legendary southern continent called Terra Australis Nondum Cognita, 'the southern land not yet known'.

French and English sailors hunted in vain for this mysterious continent until, in 1768, the British Admiralty organized the world's first scientific expedition. The aim of this voyage was to prove or disprove the continent's existence. To lead the expedition they appointed the brilliant navigator, James Cook. Cook was born on 27 October 1728 in a small village in Yorkshire. At the age of eighteen he became ship's boy on the collier *Freelove*, which ferried coal down the perilous North Sea coast to London. After five years studying astronomy and mathematics, Cook was promoted to the position of ship's mate.

Above *Ferdinand Magellan (1470–1521).*

Below *The farm worker's cottage in Yorkshire where Cook was born.*

On 17 June 1755, on the eve of England's Seven Years' War with France, Cook enlisted in the Navy. Promotion was usually given only to wealthy gentlemen, but after a month among the 60-gun *Eagle*'s largely press-ganged crew, Cook was appointed Master's-mate, and was made responsible for navigation. Within six months, he was promoted to Boatswain (Bos'n), and in 1757 became Master of the 64-gun *Pembroke*.

In Canada, Cook's excellent sounding of the St Lawrence River made possible the capture of French-held Quebec in September 1759. He then charted the lower part of the river with great precision as Master of the Admiral's flagship *Northumberland*.

Returning to London in November 1762, Cook was appointed King's Surveyor and, during the following five summers, mapped Newfoundland's coast.

In February 1768, King George III contributed £4,000 to a voyage organized by the Royal Society to carry astronomers to the Pacific. The Admiralty provided a ship, *Endeavour*, and gave forty-year-old Cook command. He was commissioned to the rank of lieutenant and handed secret papers outlining his real task, which was to try and find the mysterious southern continent, Terra Australis.

Above This engraving marks the British capture of Quebec from the French.

Below King George III of England.

The *Endeavour*

'A better ship for such service I never would wish for', was Cook's view when he took command of HMS *Endeavour* on 27 May 1768. The 360 tonne ship was a sturdy, slow-moving collier, similar to that on which Cook had been apprenticed. She was short and flat-bottomed, and could sail in waters as shallow as 5 metres.

Endeavour lay at Deptford Wharf during two months of preparation. Shipwrights covered her hull below the water line with a horsehair and tar mixture, over which thick deal planks were hammered with thousands of flat-headed nails. These would provide protection against the wood-boring, tropical 'teredo' sea-worm.

Twenty-two cannon were hauled aboard. Below deck were stored coal and lumber; gunpowder; the armourer's forge; rope and canvas; the surgeon's amputating knives and even apparatus to remove salt from sea water. There were huge barrels of food and drink: 17 tonnes of biscuit, 5 tonnes of flour, 5,455 litres of beer and 12 months' supply of salted meat. Six dozen cooped hens were taken to supply eggs, and a goat was included to provide milk for the officers.

Cook also took 2,273 litres of vinegar for scrubbing the decks, 3,628 kg of sauerkraut (pickled cabbage), wort (evaporated malt), fruit syrups and dried soups; in the belief that cleanliness and fresh food

Above *The coastal collier H.M.S Endeavour is shown here, ready for a journey across the Pacific.*

would prevent scurvy. This terrible disease, which caused 'discoloured spots...over the whole of the body, swelled legs [and] putrid gums,' commonly killed one in three sailors on ocean voyages.

There were seventy-one crew and twelve marines in the ship's company, the sailors sleeping in hammocks among the stores. When *Endeavour* sailed to Plymouth on 30 July 1768, she was further burdened by a scientific party of 'gentlemen' led by Joseph Banks of the Royal Society.

Banks, an amateur botanist who had contributed £10,000 towards the voyage, was accompanied by a naturalist, two artists, a secretary, and four servants. Lieutenant Cook watched sternly as Banks' baggage of specimen jars, books, easels, insect-catching equipment and two greyhounds came aboard.

The voyage's official purpose was to observe the path of Venus across the Sun. Cook, who had reported on an eclipse from Newfoundland in August 1766, was appointed chief astronomer and given a portable observatory, telescope and clocks. His destination was Tahiti, an island that had been visited in 1767 by Captain Samuel Wallis.

At 2.00 pm on 26 August 1768, the *Endeavour* (once manned by fifteen crew but now almost a floating village bustling with ninety-four men) embarked for the Pacific.

Below *The central figure in this engraving is the naturalist Sir Joseph Banks (1743–1820). He was the leader of a party of scientists that joined the crew of the overcrowded* Endeavour.

Tahiti

Crossing the Atlantic, the *Endeavour* made an unhappy stop at Rio de Janeiro, where the Governor accused Cook of smuggling. As they continued south, seals and penguins were sighted, and on one occasion Banks rewarded two sailors with rum for netting the thousands of butterflies that had settled on the rigging.

At Tierra del Fuego, the crew gathered 'scurvy grass' (the plant we know as cress) for their soup. Banks journeyed inland and was caught in a snowstorm in which his two servants froze to death.

Rounding Cape Horn on 27 January 1769, *Endeavour* was welcomed to the Pacific by flying-fish and a playful dolphin. Three weeks later the ship anchored off the lush, mountainous island of Tahiti. Islanders darted out to greet Cook in tiny canoes balanced with 'outriggers' and 21 m long double-canoes, lashed together beneath fighting-platforms.

Below *This map shows the routes of Captain Cook's three remarkable ocean voyages.*

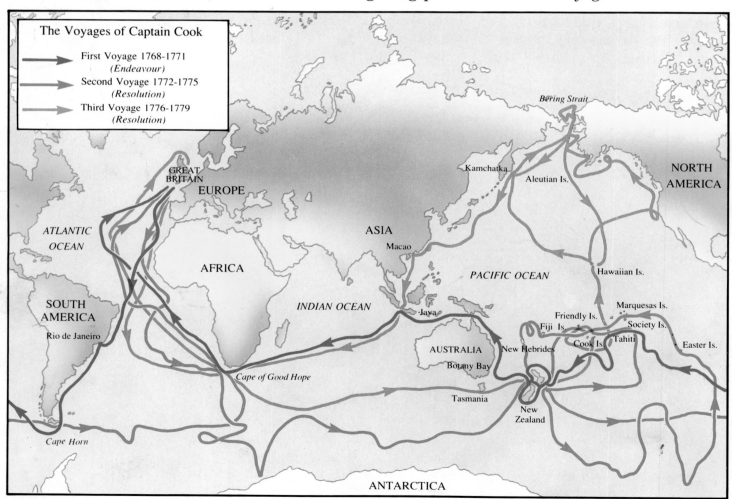

The Voyages of Captain Cook

First Voyage 1768-1771
(*Endeavour*)
Second Voyage 1772-1775
(*Resolution*)
Third Voyage 1776-1779
(*Resolution*)

Beautiful Tahitian women wearing flower garlands presented the crew with yams and coconuts. Cook ordered his men to show them, 'all imaginable humanity', and forbade the crew to offer the islanders gifts of iron or cloth from the *Endeavour*.

The Tahitians had no understanding of why the crew considered their own possessions to be their own private property. Soon the islanders showed themselves to be expert pickpockets. Attending a welcoming feast of fish and breadfruit, Cook's party lost a spy-glass and snuff-box. Cook reacted kindly. 'That thieves are hanged in England,' he wrote 'I thought no reason why they should be shot in Tahiti.' A less understanding marine, though, later killed an islander for stealing a musket.

Both Tahitian men and women decorated themselves by painfully driving dyes into their skin with sharp rocks. This lead to the practice of 'tattooing' that became fashionable among sailors. On the westerly island of Ulieta, Cook watched dancers moving to the music of nose-flutes and drums. He also witnessed funeral ceremonies conducted by a priest in a cloak of pigeon feathers and dogs'-hair, during which women beat their heads with sharks' teeth.

Above Matavai Bay, Cook built Fort Venus, from which the six-hour transit of Venus was carefully recorded on 3

June 1769. When the ship left Tahiti on 13 July, many islanders were in tears, and two marines, unwilling to leave, had to be hauled aboard in irons.

Endeavour now toured the neighbouring Society Islands, navigated by Tahitian divers, who plunged into the sea to guide her keel over perilous coral reefs. They were led by a priest named Tupaia, who remained aboard as Cook sailed north.

Above *Cook and his crew regarded Tahiti as an island paradise. This picture of the Rangiroa Atoll shows the type of lush scenery they would have seen.*

The Maoris

Cook now informed the ship's company of his secret orders to discover Terra Australis, and turned south. The *Endeavour* plunged through the endless and stormy ocean to 40 degrees latitude, but the only land sighted turned out to be cloud.

The expedition remained free from scurvy. Cook had given two men a dozen lashes for refusing fresh beef, and tricked the crew into demanding the sauerkraut by serving it only to the officers. Burning coals cleared stale air from below decks, and the ship's woodwork was 'cured' by scrubbing it with vinegar and gunpowder.

Cook turned west, and on 7 October 1769 Ship's-boy Nick Young sighted New Zealand's uncharted north-eastern coast. The local Maoris tried to steal the landing-party's pinnace, but fled when one was killed by musket-fire. Cook intercepted a Maori canoe, intending to show his friendship, but the Maoris attacked and three of them were then killed. 'Thus ended',

Below *Launching their war canoes from New Zealand's coast, Maori warriors taunted and challenged the* Endeavour's *crew.*

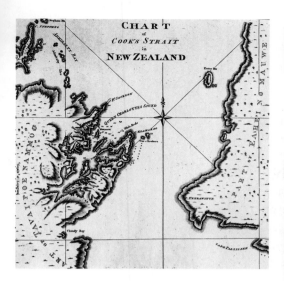

wrote Banks, 'the most disagreeable day my life has yet seen.'

The Tahitian priest Tupaia eventually calmed the Maoris. They understood his language, but were far more war-like and bloodthirsty than the Tahitians. Large war canoes, each containing up to one hundred warriors, approached *Endeavour*, their prows carved with terrifying faces. The warriors carried clubs and wore jade earrings and necklaces shaped like their gods. Their hair was scraped back with combs and hung with feathers, and their faces were decorated with tattoos.

To challenge Cook, the Maoris chanted taunts and performed a violent war-dance, 'admirably calculated to strike Terror into their enemies.' The friendly Maori greeting, though, was to rub noses.

Sailing north from 'Poverty Bay', Cook circled the island. The people were awestruck when they saw the English sailors rowing backwards,

believing they must have eyes in the backs of their skulls.

At Queen Charlotte's Sound in the south-west, Maoris fished with baited basket-nets of woven grass, and occasionally hurled stones at *Endeavour*. When trading pieces of cloth for giant lobsters, Cook was horrified to learn that some of the Maoris were cannibals, having recently, 'killed and eaten a boat's crew of their enemies.'

On 22 January 1770, the expedition discovered Cook's Strait, which divides New Zealand in two. Cook circled both of New Zealand's islands, proving that neither was connected to the mythical Southern Continent. Banks gathered 400 new plants while Cook charted New Zealand's 3,860 km coastline in astonishing detail. On 1 April 1770 *Endeavour* departed from Cape Farewell.

Above left On discovering the stretch of water that divides New Zealand into two islands, the expedition named it Cook's Strait.

Above right The beautiful bay of Queen Charlotte's Sound, where Cook traded with the Maoris for giant lobsters.

Shipwreck

Far right *In the safety of a sheltered bay, Endeavour underwent two months of repairs.*

Left *A painting of Cook's historic landing at Botany Bay, Australia.*

Below *Navigating Australia's north-eastern coast, Endeavour was nearly ship-wrecked on the dangerous coral of the Great Barrier Reef.*

Extending his homeward voyage once more, Cook steered the battered *Endeavour* west towards Tasmania. A gale altered her course, and on 19 April 1770, Lieutenant Hicks sighted a sparse, rocky shore lashed by a huge surf. It was the unexplored east coast of Australia. Cook called his anchorage Stingray Harbour after the fish that lived there in abundance.

Two Aborigines bravely hurled javelins at the 40-man landing party before retreating under musket-fire, abandoning their bark-built canoes. Banks found so many different plants growing along the inlet that Cook renamed this natural harbour Botany Bay.

Charting north-west, Cook entered the jaws of the Great Barrier Reef, where submerged teeth of jagged coral guard 1,930 km of Australia's north-east coast. On the night of 11 June, with a terrible grating noise, *Endeavour* struck the reef. Cook woke, rushed on deck and calmly issued orders. Anchors were lowered, and ballast, six cannons and tonnes of rotten stores, were cast overboard.

The reef tore a deep hole in *Endeavour's* hull, and officers, crew and gentlemen desperately manned three water-pumps. At low tide, only the collier's flat bottom kept her from capsizing.

Nearly twenty-four hours later, by heaving on her anchor chains, the crew hauled *Endeavour* free. She was patched by fothering (hauling a sail, water-proofed with wool, oakum and dung, beneath her leaking hull) to mend any holes. When *Endeavour* limped into a bay, a piece of coral was found to have lodged in the largest hole, miraculously preventing the ship from sinking.

While the carpenter repaired *Endeavour*, Banks marvelled at giant sea-turtles, and ant-hills as tall as a man. He was amazed when a creature resembling, 'a wild dog but for its running in which it jumped like a hare or deer', outpaced his greyhounds. When one of the fantastic animals was shot and eaten, he learnt that the Aborigines called it a 'kangaru'.

Two months later, a rowing boat taking soundings to measure the water's depth, guided *Endeavour* into open sea, where the wind suddenly

died. The 'leadsman' dropped a line 140 fathoms without finding the sea-bed, showing the reef to be a coral wall rising from what seemed to be a bottomless ocean. Unable to anchor, *Endeavour* drifted helplessly towards it.

Catching a sudden gust of wind, Cook guided *Endeavour* through a narrow channel to anchor safely within the reef once more.

Above *The first sightings of kangaroos caused great excitement among the* Endeavour's *crew.*

The Seagoing Clock

Emerging from the Barrier Reef through Endeavour Strait into the Indian Ocean, Cook named this part of eastern Australia New South Wales. From the island of New Guinea he sailed to the disease-ridden port of Batavia, in the Dutch East Indies.

Tupaia and six other members of the crew died from disease while *Endeavour* underwent repair. Twenty-five more had become ill before the coast of England was sighted on 10 July 1771. After two years and eleven months spent at sea, fifty-six men returned alive. The ship's goat, which had also sailed with Wallis when he explored Tahiti, had completed its second voyage around the world!

In the greatest Pacific expedition to date, Cook had charted 8,050 km of coastline, cast doubts over Terra Australis' existence, and kept his entire crew free from scurvy. When presented to King George III of England, Cook was promoted to Commander. It was Banks, though, with his magnificent animal and plant collections, who received great public acclaim.

After exactly a year at home, Cook embarked again from Plymouth on 13 July 1772. He aimed to sail into the stormy southern reaches of the Pacific, where Terra Australis might lie. He would explore the icy Antarctic, retreating in winter to the islands he had not

Below *Cook departed for his second expedition from Plymouth, Devon, which was historically an important British trading port.*

Left *This picture shows H.M.S Resolution,* the last ship to be placed under Cook's command.

Below *Cook used a compass like this to help him to navigate on his second and third voyages.*

reached on his earlier first voyage. Learning from his near disastrous encounter with the Barrier Reef, Cook used two ships this time, both of which were converted Whitby colliers. He commanded the 460 tonne *Resolution*, with 91 crew and 20 marines; while the 67 crew and 12 marines of the 330 tonne *Adventure* sailed under Tobias Furneaux. The crew included two sailors who had worked on whaling vessels and were experienced in navigating through ice-packed waters.

Provisions including 2 years' stores, took up so much space that Cook had to replace the sea-chests with duffel bags.

For his party of sixteen, including two musicians, Banks had ordered an extra deck to be built on the *Resolution*. Cook promptly removed it, as it badly over-balanced the ship, and Banks immediately withdrew from the expedition. His place was taken by a quarrelsome scientist, J R Forster, his son George, and landscape painter William Hodges.

This was the first Pacific expedition to use a chronometer. To fix a ship's longitude precisely, a navigator needs to keep time accurately. Most clocks, though, became unreliable at sea, because their metal parts grew larger and smaller with the changing temperatures. John Harrison solved this problem by using a balance made of brass and steel, which kept his clock ticking steadily. Cook was equipped with a copy of Harrison's sea clock, called a chronometer, which he called a, 'Watch Machine . . . our never failing guide.'

Islands of Ice

After taking on stores at the island of Madeira and at Capetown in South Africa, Cook sailed south for the unexplored Antarctic. His two ships were soon coated with ice and were rolling in polar gales. Inch-long icicles hung from the sailors' noses, and their hands often froze to the rigging ropes which had set like iron. Cook issued heavy jackets and trousers, made of canvas and wool, and red woollen caps, and he ordered extra brandy rations.

Waves of over 18 m crashed over mountains of ice, some 3 km around. *Resolution* neared one great iceberg, Cook believing it to be a cliff. Both crews watched a cluster of penguins march across an ice-floe like well-drilled soldiers. The expedition entered a heavy mist, so thick it obscured the bowsprit. When it eventually lifted, it revealed whales coasting beside the ships.

On 17 January 1773, the expedition crossed the

Below *Freezing conditions and islands of floating ice made Cook's approach to the Antarctic a difficult one.*

Antarctic Circle. Pack ice finally forced Cook to turn north-east, only 121 km from Antarctica's coast. In a perilous operation, piles of ice were hauled out of the ocean, and melted for drinking water.

In a dense February fog, Cook lost contact with *Adventure*. After firing guns and lighting signal beacons without success, he turned east towards New Zealand.

Resolution now entered a fantastic landscape of 'ice islands'. One 90 m high berg slowly turned right over as the ship passed; another shattered suddenly like glass. Smaller ice-blocks occasionally thudded into the ship's hull.

Cook put into New Zealand's Dusky Sound on 27 March 1773, after 117 days at sea. He traded with the Maoris and gathered provisions. Five weeks later Cook departed for Queen Charlotte's Sound, where whirlwinds cast up six water-spouts to greet him. Furneaux was already anchored there. Several of his men were sick from scurvy, and Cook ordered them to eat his strict diet of wild celery and other fresh food.

Ever impatient, Cook departed east in June, as the South Pacific winter set in. He called it a, 'season by no means favourable for discoveries'.

In August 1773, Cook received an emotional welcome at Tahiti. While the islanders clambered aboard, *Resolution* drifted in the calm on to a reef. Each wave dashed the ship against the coral with a sickening thud until finally, the anchor caught fast.

Cook sailed on to the Society Islands where gifts of fruits and hogs soon filled *Resolution* and *Adventure's* decks. Two of the islanders, Omai and Odiddy, accompanied the expedition when it departed in September.

The Furthest South

Cook was so warmly welcomed at the beautiful Tonga Islands in October 1773 that he called them the Friendly Islands. The Tongans eagerly traded feathers from the red-breasted musk parrot for nails. Cook noticed that many of the local people had joints of their fingers missing, having chopped them off in sacrifice to their gods.

Sailing to New Zealand, *Resolution* and *Adventure* were separated again by a violent storm. *Resolution* left Queen Charlotte's Sound alone, and zig-zagged through the Antarctic. On 30 January 1774, Cook reached Latitude 71° 10', his furthest point south.

Midshipman George Vancouver clambered along the bowsprit waving his hat, to ensure that he was the nearest man ever to the South Pole.

For four days *Resolution* anchored off Easter Island. 20 km long, barren, and isolated in a vast, empty ocean, it was the loneliest of spots with mysterious stone statues towering over its shores. Its islanders demonstrated a strange form of writing on wooden slabs.

Passing the Marquesas Islands, the expedition returned to Matavai Bay, where they became the only Europeans to have seen Tahiti's war-fleet set sail.

Streamers and flags fluttered from 330 canoes, many of which were double-hulled and one of which was as long as *Resolution*. Thousands of warriors, carrying clubs, spears and stones and wearing, 'Cloth, Turbands, Breast Plates

Above *The strange stone statues which stand on the barren slopes of Rano Raraku, Easter Island seemed to stare at the sailors.*

and Helmets,' crowded their fighting platforms.

After sweeping past the Society Islands and Tonga, Cook spent six weeks charting the New Hebrides. He went ashore alone waving a green branch of friendship, but the Melanesians were hostile. At Erromanga he was met with a hail of stones and arrows as the inhabitants tried to haul his boat ashore. On Tanna, a southerly island, Cook witnessed Yasur Volcano, which, 'made a terrible noise throwing up...columns of smoke and fire at every

eruption.' The islanders believed that a clumsy evil spirit spilled the lava when playing underground with red-hot stones.

Sailing for New Zealand, Cook reached New Caledonia, the fourth largest Pacific island, and Norfolk Island, where convicts were to be imprisoned in later years.

On 18 October 1774, *Resolution* anchored again in Queen Charlotte's Sound. Here, Cook later learned, Maoris had murdered ten of Furneaux's men and then eaten them.

Above *Fighting broke out when the Melanesians of Erromanga attempted to capture Cook's landing craft.*

The Final Voyage

Resolution reached England on 30 July 1775, a year after Furneaux's return. Assisted by his chronometer, Cook had charted thirty islands, previously unmapped by Europeans. If Terra Australis existed it consisted only of frozen wasteland.

Cook was promoted to Captain and elected into the Royal Society, receiving the Copley Medal, its highest award. After over three years at sea, not one of *Resolution's* men had died from scurvy. Cook took a well-paid post at Greenwich Hospital, but soon grew restless. When the Earl of Sandwich, First Lord of the Admiralty, asked him to recommend a commander for a voyage to seek the Northwest Passage, Cook volunteered himself.

Merchants had long searched for a sea-route around North America from the Pacific to the Atlantic, through which tea and spices from Asia could be carried to Britain. Many explorers had investigated America's Atlantic coast for this Northwest Passage, but Cook intended to seek its entrance in the Pacific.

On 12 July 1776, Cook sailed from Plymouth in *Resolution*. His crew included William Bligh, later victim of the famous Mutiny on the Bounty, and Omai the Society Islander.

King George III had supplied the expedition with cattle, goats, pigs, sheep and rabbits for breeding in distant lands. Cats and dogs also wandered *Resolution's* decks and Cook called his departing ship, 'A Noah's Ark'.

Above *Greenwich Hospital, where Cook was given a post between his second and third voyages.*

Above *John Montagu, fourth Earl of Sandwich.*

A second vessel, the 290 tonne collier *Discovery* with a ship's-company of ninety-two commanded by Charles Clerke, joined Cook at Cape Town.

Resolution was leaking before Cook reached Tasmania. Timber had to be cut to replace her mast, destroyed by storms, and one sailor complained: 'If I return in *Resolution*...I may safely Venture in a Ship Built of Ginger Bread.'

The continuous chirp of insects called cicadas welcomed Cook back to Queen Charlotte's Sound. He found crops they had planted on the previous voyage growing well, and he left rabbits and goats with the Maoris.

After slowly navigating the Cook Islands, the expedition reached the Tongas in April 1777. Cook spent eleven weeks there, refreshing his stores and allowing the livestock to feed on fresh grass. The Tongan men performed a swaying 'paddle dance', and 100 warriors performed marches which put Cook's marines to shame. The women danced also, and gave exciting displays of boxing.

Cook, once so determined to explore, did not want to sail on to Fiji and Samoa, which were known to be 5 km away. His temper was growing short as the strain of seven years of seafaring was showing.

Below *The crews of* Resolution *and* Discovery *were entertained on Tonga by the local warriors' swaying paddle dance.*

The Sandwich Islands

Cook received a great welcome at Tahiti in August 1777. Provisions were bought for red feathers which the Tahitians prized higher than iron. Gifts were presented to Cook by a girl wearing so much cloth around her hips that she looked almost as wide as she was tall. During a religious ceremony witnessed by the expedition, Tahitian priests made a human sacrifice to their gods.

On hearing that Cook was suffering from rheumatic pains caused by his damp quarters on the leaking ship, a chief sent out a canoe containing twelve women. Laying Cook upon a blanket, they pummelled and kneaded his aching flesh brutally. 'They made my bones crack!' Cook complained, but found that after the massage his pains had vanished.

Touring the Society Islands, Cook continued to show flashes of temper. He burned houses and canoes on Moorea while searching for a missing goat. On Juahine, a thief who had stolen a sextant was punished by having his hair and ears cut off.

After unloading much of his livestock and returning a tearful Omai to his people, Cook said his last goodbye to the Society Islands.

Sailing north, the expedition reached an uninhabited island on 24 December, which they named Christmas Island. The crew feasted on delicious turtles. Their meat was almost exhausted when, on 18 January 1778, Cook chanced upon three uncharted islands. They were Oahu, Kanai and Niihau, part of the Hawaiian group, which Cook called the Sandwich Islands.

Volcanoes smouldered in the distance, and tall, beautifully carved wooden figures stood guard beside religious 'morai'

temples on black ash beaches. The laughing Hawaiians carried out hogs and sweet potatoes in handsome canoes, to trade for nails, and Cook noted, 'We again found ourselves in the land of plenty.'

Some islanders, though, soon attempted to steal the leadsman's line and the butcher's cleaver, and in one tragic incident Lt Williamson shot a man dead.

The Hawaiians were as at home in the sea as on land. As well as being remarkable swimmers, they skimmed over the tall waves 'with an incredible Swiftness' on narrow wooden planks, similar to present-day surfboards. Ashore, the women performed the hip-swaying 'hula' dance.

Cook's arrival in Hawaii greatly excited the local priests. Wearing masks decorated with foliage and strips of bark, they performed ceremonies for Lono, an ancient god of happiness and fruitfulness, who they believed would one day return to the islands. Cook was astonished when the islanders fell flat at his feet, but thought it was just a greeting for a great chief. The Hawaiians, however, believed that Captain Cook was their god.

The Singing Welcome

Cook left the Sandwich Islands on 2 February 1778. Sailing north-east for a month he sighted the misty west coast of America, then called New Albion, now known as the coast of Oregon. He named its stormy headland Cape Foulweather.

On 29 March, *Resolution* and *Discovery* anchored in Nootka Sound, in what is now Vancouver Island, British Columbia. Many inlets disappeared here into pine-covered mountain slopes. Albatrosses and a bald eagle soared overhead, and the wings of tiny humming-birds buzzed noisily.

Local people soon began to approach the ships, paddling dug-out canoes 12m long with a huge bird's head painted on their chief's craft. Their faces were smeared with red and black grease, and their long hair decorated with feathers, seaweed and bark strips. One man suddenly stood up, wildly shaking two rattles and howling. His companions threw red dust into the water and he scattered handfuls of white feathers. Drumming leaf-shaped oars against their canoes, the local Nootka people chanted and sang powerfully.

Below *The singing of the inhabitants of Nootka Sound welcomed Cook's expedition to North America.*

The music of the Native Americans made a strong impression on Cook.

Visiting their wooden long-houses, Cook noted the gaping faces of 'monstrous carved posts', or 'totem-poles'. In exchange for copper kettles, nails and shirt-buttons, the sailors obtained the otter and beaver skins, that would help to strengthen North America's fur trade.

After replacing *Resolution's* rotten masts and rigging, the expedition departed. The local people sang farewell, and dancers put on terrifying carved masks of animal and bird faces.

At Prince William Sound, Alaska, the local people, bearded and hidden beneath sealskin overcoats, conical hats and bearpaw mittens resembled great bears. One frightened member of the crew swore that these people must have two mouths. This was because of the way they had slit their lips and inserted decorated bones into the wounds.

At Cook Inlet, the expedition sailed 241 km up what they hoped was the Northwest Passage. It was just a river. Retreating, they sailed through the Aleutian Islands into the Bering Sea, then navigated the narrow Bering Strait that divides America and Asia. Crossing the Arctic Circle on 14 August 1778, Cook met a wall of ice. The crew slaughtered long-tusked, barking walruses for oil and

meat, but few shared Cook's taste for this food.

Ice soon forced the leaking *Resolution* to turn back towards Unalaska, where the crew gathered fish and berries, and rode the dog-sleds used there by both natives and Russian fur-traders.

Above *Walruses, such as these living on the Arctic ice, were killed by Cook's crew for their meat.*

Death of a God

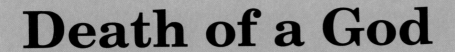

Sailing from Unalaska, the expedition sighted the Sandwich Islands again on 25 November 1778. Now Cook reached and charted the largest of the group, Hawaii itself.

On 17 January 1779, Cook anchored in Kealakekua Bay which the Hawaiian priests called 'the path of the gods'. The islanders welcomed him with uncontrolled excitement, 'swimming about the Ship like shoals of fish,' and launching a fleet of 1,000 canoes trailing white banners.

A priest named Koa came aboard and presented Cook with a fly-whisk, hogs and fruits, and draped a red cloak about his shoulders. Cook was presented to Terreeoboo, King of Hawaii, and escorted to ceremonies in the sacred morais, unaware that the priests were worshipping him as their returning god Lono.

On 1 February 1779, one of *Resolution's* sailors died and was buried on Hawaii. The islanders' behaviour suddenly

changed. They had lavished so many gifts of food on the English, that they were going hungry themselves. Thieving increased and the Hawaiians urged the sailors to leave.

The expedition departed on 4 February, but sailed straight into a storm. *Resolution's* mast split, her old leaks re-opened, and Cook turned reluctantly back to Kealakekua Bay. This time there was no welcome.

On the night of 13 February, the Hawaiians stole *Discovery's* cutter. A furious Cook landed with two boats. Marching ashore with Lieutenant Phillips and nine marines, he seized King Terreeoboo, as hostage for the stolen cutter. On the journey to the beach, though, the king was begged by his wife and chiefs not to go. Confused, old Terreeoboo just sat down, trembling.

Some 2,000 islanders quickly gathered around, murmuring and blowing on conch-shells. Glaring angrily at the massed islanders, Cook ordered a withdrawal. Then news arrived that further along the coast sailors had killed a chief.

A warrior raised a spear, tipped with a gift of iron from the *Resolution*, and Cook fired a shot which bounced off his matting armour. He shot again, and a Hawaiian fell. The marines opened fire, and the islanders hurled a hail of stones.

Against the incredible noise of the Hawaiians' screams, Cook turned and strolled towards the sea, at a strangely slow pace. A warrior struck him hesitantly with a club, and Cook fell to his knees. The chief Ku'a then plunged a knife into Cook's neck, again and again, and the shrieking islanders fell upon him.

Incredibly, Cook raised his head and stared back at his ships. Lt Williamson, though, was rowing his landing pinnace away, leaving Cook to die at the hands of the Hawaiians.

The Legacy of Cook

The Hawaiians burnt the bodies of Cook and four marines during the night. A week later a sorrowful chief returned Cook's remains. They were identified by a scar on one hand, caused by an explosion in Newfoundland fifteen years earlier.

The islanders cleared the bay on 21 February and Cook's remains were buried at sea, flags flying at half-mast and ten guns firing a salute.

The expedition recrossed the Bering Strait under Clerke's command, to search again for the Northwest Passage. Ice once more barred the way, forcing the ships back to Kamchatka, Siberia. From here the Russians sent word of Cook's death to England. Newspapers published the sad news six months before *Resolution* and *Discovery* arrived home in October 1780.

The British people mourned Cook, but many failed to recognize what he had actually achieved. He had, after all, never found Terra Australis or the Northwest Passage, but only disproved their existence.

Cook was both the first to use a chronometer for accurate charting and to defeat disease at sea. With fewer people dying during a voyage, less crew were needed, and so smaller ships were soon designed.

Cook showed an unusual concern for the people of the lands he explored. He realized the appearance of Europeans would often, 'serve only to disturb that happy tranquillity they and their forefathers had enjoyed.' In 1788, the Aborigines watched the first shipment of convicts land at Botany Bay. In 1797, the first missionaries arrived in Tahiti.

Above The information collected on Cook's incredible voyages earned him a place among history's greatest navigators.

Left Cook Island, also known as Rarotonga, is one of many places in the world where the names commemorate Cook's discoveries.

Below Captain Cook's charting of new lands led to the building of settlements such as this one at Sydney Cove, Australia in 1798.

A plaque in Kealakekua Bay, which is submerged beneath the Pacific Ocean at high tide, commemorates Cook's death. The names of New Zealand's Cook Strait, the Polynesian Cook Islands, and Cook Inlet, Alaska, provide more fitting monuments to his remarkable voyages.

Cook's exploration of so many distant lands, and his detailed charting of islands such as New Zealand and Australia, which others had merely visited, justify Lord Palliser's view of him as, 'The ablest and most renowned navigator this or any other country hath produced.' By removing the cloak of mystery that had covered the Pacific, Cook left his greatest legacy – a completed map of the world. He once wrote: 'I had ambition not only to go further than

any man had been before, but as far as it was possible for man to go.'

Glossary

Aborigines A people living in Australia from earliest known times.

Amputating knives The special instruments used by surgeons when cutting through bones to remove a limb.

Armourer Someone who makes or mends weapons and armour.

Astronomy The study of planets and stars. This was highly important in early navigational techniques.

Atoll A ring-shaped coral reef enclosing a lagoon.

Berg A huge, floating chunk of ice.

Boatswain (Bos'n) The officer in charge of a ship's sails and rigging. It was the boatswain who was responsible for calling sailors to duty.

Botanist Someone who studies plants.

Bow The rounded front of a ship.

Bowsprit The stout pole extending forward from a ship's bows.

Cannibal Someone who eats human flesh.

Chronometer A clock which keeps accurate time, despite different temperatures at sea.

Collier A ship designed to transport coal.

Coral A colourful underwater growth which is created by the skeletons and deposits of sea creatures.

Cutter A boat carried by a larger vessel which is used to transport passengers or light cargo to shore.

Deal A plank (or planks) made from softwood such as fir or pine.

Duffel bag A cylindrical canvas bag often used by sailors.

Eclipse The effect caused when one planet blocks out the light of another by passing in front of it.

Forge A furnace for softening metal before shaping it to make tools, armour, and so on.

Hull The frame of a ship.

Keel The bottom of a ship.

Latitude The distance of a point north or south from the Equator.

Leadsman A sailor who casts lead weight over the side of a ship to measure the depth of sea.

Longitude The distance of a point east or west from the Greenwich Meridian.

Lumber Wood that has been sawn into boards.

Maori A member of the people living in New Zealand since before the arrival of European settlers.

Marine A soldier who has been trained to fight on land or sea.

Master The officer responsible for navigating a ship.

Mate The officer next in line to the Master.

Matting Armour Strong clothing made from fabric. This was used by soldiers to protect their bodies during battle.

Naturalist Someone who studies animals or plants.

Navigator Someone who guides the course of the ship.

Outrigger A beam attached to the side of a canoe which is used to help it balance.

Pickpocket Someone who steals from people's pockets or bags.

Pinnace A small boat carried as part of the equipment used by a large boat.

Press-ganged Forced to join the Army or Navy by a gang of thugs.

Prow The pointed front of a ship.

Reef A ridge of rock, sand or coral hidden just below the surface of the water. This is very hazardous to ships, as it may easily cause them to run aground.

Rigging A ship's ropes.

Royal Society An association founded in the seventeenth century to encourage the study of science.

Scurvy A disease, often fatal, caused by a lack of vitamin C.

Sextant A navigational instrument.

Snuff box A box designed to hold a sort of powdered tobacco which is taken into the body by sniffing.

Sounding The method used to find the depth of the water by dropping a weighted line.

Spy glass A small telescope.

Tattoo Ink marks permanently printed into the skin with sharp stones or needles. The faces of the Maoris Cook met were covered in tattoos.

Finding Out More

Sydney Parkinson's paintings of Cook's voyages can be seen at the Natural History Museum, London. Many of Cook's navigational instruments, paintings and models of his ships, and many of the original paintings made on the voyages can be seen at the National Maritime Museum in London. Here, Cook's original chronometer still keeps accurate time.

Books to Read

Your local library will be able to help you to find some of these books:

A Blackwood, *Captain Cook* (Wayland, 1986)

J Fagan, *Captain Cook. His Artists, His Voyages* (Daily Telegraph, 1970)

R Hough, *The Murder of Captain Cook* (Macmillan, 1979)

A Langley, *The First Men Around the World* (Wayland, 1983)

R Syme, *The Travels of Captain Cook* (Michael Joseph, 1972)

D Wilcox, *Explorers* (BBC Publications, 1975)

Picture Acknowledgements

The publishers would like to thank the following for allowing their illustrations to be used in this book:

The Bridgeman Art Library 20 (top); Mary Evans Picture Library 7, 13 (bottom), 14, 17 (top), 25, 29 (top & bottom); The Mansell Collection 4 (bottom), 6, 20 (bottom); Peter Newark's Western Americana *frontispiece*, 4 (top), 5 (bottom), 12 (top); Tony Stone Worldwide 9, 11 (right), 12 (bottom), 18; and Topham Picture Library 5 (top), 15 (top & bottom), 17 (bottom), 28. All other illustrations are from the Wayland Picture Library. The map on page 8 is by Peter Bull.

Index